Grammar B

GW00493709

Contents

unit 1

Sentences

🔑 Key idea

A sentence is a group of words that makes sense on its own.
A sentence starts with a capital letter and finishes with a full stop.

capital letter

My best friend will be eight at the end of
this month. She is planning a big party.

full stop   capital letter   full stop

⭐ Top Tip

Sentences make sense
of what you read.
Sentences make sense
of what you write.

Try it out! ••••••••••••••••••••••••

**Copy out these words. Make them into sentences by putting in the
capital letters at the start and the full stops at the end.** *(1 mark for
each correct answer)*

1 there are thirty children in our class
2 our teacher can be very funny
3 he tells us a joke if we finish our work early
4 one day he was worried that we would not stop laughing
5 he said that the noise would be too much for him

• •

There are two sentences on each line. Can you find them? Write them out, putting a full stop at the end of the first sentence and a capital letter at the start of the second sentence. The first one has been done for you. *(1 mark for each correct answer)*

1 My teacher told us this joke it is about a swimming lesson.
  My teacher told us this joke. It is about a swimming lesson.
2 A teacher took his class to the pool he wanted to teach swimming.
3 He told everyone to do breaststroke one boy did backstroke.
4 The teacher then asked his pupils to do the crawl the boy continued to do the backstroke.
5 The teacher could not understand why the boy would only do the backstroke the boy smiled.
6 He said he had just finished lunch he did not want to swim on a full stomach!

Take up the challenge! •

There are ten mistakes here, so it is hard to tell where one sentence finishes and the next one starts. Write out the paragraph, putting in the missing capital letters and full stops. *(1 mark for each correct answer)*

the best girl at sport in my class is my best friend. last year she won two medals for swimming It was when we had a huge swimming gala at the baths in town. everyone in the lower school was there, and their parents. the noise was so loud that our teacher nearly went deaf There was a race for all the girls in our year My best friend won the race by two whole metres. the last race was for girls and boys. all the girls were screaming for my friend She managed to win by the tips of her fingers.

Using commas in a list

 Key idea

Commas can be used to separate items in a list.

Alison, Michael, Alex and Naomi were quadruplets.

comma   comma

Commas make the sentence easier to understand.

The last two items in a list are often separated by a word such as **and** or **or** so a comma is not needed.

Try it out! ●●●●●●●●●●●●●●●●●●●●●●●●●●●●●●●●●●

Write these sentences correctly. Make sure that commas are put in the correct places. Each sentence needs two commas. *(1 mark for each correct comma)*

1 The quadruplets had identical coats scarves hats and bags.
2 That was fine when they were babies toddlers pre-school or infants.
3 Adults thought they looked sweet cute different and amusing.
4 It was not fine adorable suitable or cool when they were older.
5 Other children smiled pointed laughed and giggled.

Some of the items in these lists are phrases, not single words. You must be careful to put the commas in the correct places. Write these out, putting two commas in each sentence. The first one has been done for you. *(1 mark for each correct comma)*

1 The children's mother talked persuaded begged desperately and shouted angrily about their food.
  The children's mother talked, persuaded, begged desperately and shouted angrily about their food.

2 Alison Michael Alex and Naomi were all very fussy eaters.
3 Alison had beans beans on toast beans with egg or beans and chips.
4 Michael demanded fried chicken chicken and chips chicken nuggets or chicken croquettes.
5 Alex had boiled eggs scrambled eggs poached eggs or fried eggs.
6 Naomi had to have chips chips and tomato sauce chip sandwiches or chips with vinegar.

This is a muddle because commas have been forgotten or put in the wrong places. Correct the ten mistakes. *(1 mark for each correct comma)*

Alison Michael, Alex and Naomi were fed up. Everyone, had stared laughed or pointed at their clothes. They would get revenge, and fun with their lunches. They went to the hall to order four drinks four, meals and four puddings. The quadruplets put chips on Alison's plate egg on Naomi's plate beans on Michael's plate and chicken on Alex's, plate. Three children two teachers and the head teacher called them the wrong names. It was a great trick! Then ...

unit 3

Question marks and exclamation marks

 Key idea

A question mark looks like **?** It comes at the end of a sentence that asks a question.

Is that hot question mark

An exclamation mark looks like **!** It comes at the end of sentence that shows strong feeling or emotion, or is shouted.

Ouch! Don't touch! exclamation mark

exclamation mark

⭐ **Top Tip**

Remember, you don't have to put a full stop after **?** and **!** The full stop is built in!

Try it out! •

All of these sentences need ? or ! at the end. Decide which and copy them out correctly.

(1 mark for each correct answer)

1 Would Ahmed's mother let him go to the football club
2 How could he persuade her
3 He had it
4 He was so clever
5 He would please her by cleaning the floor
6 Where was the mop kept
7 Grab it quickly
8 Where was the washing stuff
9 Swoosh it around
10 Off we go

Write these sets of words in the correct order to make a question or an exclamation. To give you a clue, the first word has a capital letter and the last word has a question mark or an exclamation mark. The first one is done for you. (*1 mark for each correct answer*)

1   the washing Was well? going
    Was the washing going well?

2   the floor Did cleaner? look any

3   he need Did water? more

4   disaster! what a Oh

5   slipped! The had bucket

6   someone! me Help

7   water? How can rid I get this of

8   me Get brigade! the fire

9   mop The has skidded!

10 flooded! has kitchen The

11 Ahmed Could up clear before came? mum his

Top Tip

If a sentence asks for an answer, it needs a question mark at the end.

This story writer does not know about question marks and exclamation marks. Sometimes he has used full stops instead of them. Write this paragraph, replacing ten full stops with question marks or exclamation marks to find out what Ahmed's mother said. (*1 mark for each correct answer*)

"Help. Help. We're underwater. What has happened. There has been no mention of a flood in the weather reports. The monsoon season is over. What can it be. Got it. Ahmed. Get over here, Ahmed. Explain yourself. How did my kitchen become a muddy river. Do you know anything about it."

unit 4

Verbs in sentences

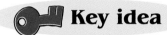

Key idea

Every sentence needs a verb.
A verb is a doing, being or having word.

The man slurped his soup. (doing)
The man was noisy. (being)
The man had soup. (having)

A verb can be a single word (**help**) or a group of words (**is helping, will be helping**).

Try it out! •

Find the verb in these sentences and write it out. Remember that it may be more than one word. *(1 mark for each correct answer)*

1   Class 3 wanted a trip out of school.
2   They longed for an overnight stay.
3   Their teacher, Miss Doyle, had promised an exciting excursion.
4   They would go to an educational residential centre in Dorset.
5   The owners of the centre ran pottery, riding, trampolining, football, basketball and cookery classes.
6   It all seemed brilliant!
7   Miss Doyle had visited the centre in her half-term holiday.
8   She had made a whistle-stop tour of the facilities.
9   The facilities sounded quite amazing.
10 Miss Doyle would be writing to all the parents.

Work in pairs. Think of two ways to perform each of these actions. Try them out and then think of the verbs for those actions. Write a sentence for each verb. For example, "writing your name" could be: I **scribbled** my name. I **signed** my name. *(1 mark for each sentence)*

1 speaking to a friend
2 getting up from your chair
3 putting down your pen
4 using a book
5 going from one side of the room to the other

 Top Tip
Read a sentence out loud to see if it makes sense.

Plans for the trip are not going well. Miss Doyle has rushed her letter to the parents. As a result, she has not written complete sentences. Verbs are sometimes wrong or missed out. Find the problems, and write out the paragraph, using the correct verb forms. (*1 mark for each correct answer*)

Class 3 going to Dorset. There only 35 spaces available on the trip. Places will to the first pupils to bring back signed forms. The trip costing £48, which is a real bargain. The pupils staying two nights, and they will all sleep in comfortable dormitories. The trip will be leading by Miss Doyle, their teacher. Two student teachers and an assistant will helping her. There to be so many activities, that the pupils to learn a great deal. It be a wonderful experience.

Write the second, correct paragraph of Miss Doyle's letter for her. Underline the verbs that you use.

unit 5
Verb tenses

Key idea

The **tense** of a verb tells you **when** the action takes place.

There are three main verb tenses:

- Past tense: I **scored** a goal last season.
- Present tense: I **score** a goal in almost every match.
- Future tense: I **will score** hat-tricks next year!

Regular past tenses end in –ed, but there are many irregular verbs to watch out for, for example:

> present tense   past tense
> Today is warm, but yesterday was cold.

> ⭐ **Top Tip**
>
> Regular past tenses end in –ed, but there are many irregular verbs to watch out for.

Try it out! • • • • • • • • • • • • • • • • • • •

Find and write out the verbs in these sentences. Write out their tenses too. *(1 mark for each correct answer)*

1 Class 3's residential trip to Dorset starts today.
verb = starts, tense = present

2 Miss Doyle will have responsibility for everything.
3 Miss Doyle felt sick with worry yesterday.
4 Today, at least at the moment, she feels better.
5 She is looking rather green and weak though.
6 The coach journey will be very difficult for her.

Choose a time phrase from the chart below and pair it up with the appropriate verb form to make a sentence. For example:

time phrase: **during the journey** + verb form: **will stop**
= **During the journey** to the hostel, we **will stop** for a snack.

Make up five sentences of your own choosing a different time phrase and verb form for each one. Your sentences can be about **school trips.** *(2 marks for each sentence)*

time phrases	verb forms
these days	will stop
when I was small	will buy
for one day every year	went
at my age	stayed
during the journey	enjoy
this year	am reading
once	

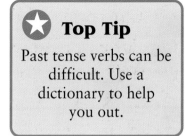

Top Tip

Past tense verbs can be difficult. Use a dictionary to help you out.

Miss Doyle is in Dorset. She is writing a postcard back to the school. Can you make sense of it? Copy it out and correct the ten mistakes she has made with verb tenses. *(1 mark for each correct answer)*

The journey is being not too bad. Only seven children will be sick on the way here. I will think that was what will happen: I cannot be sure because I was sick myself. Darren, the student teacher, will be wonderful: he looks after all of us and makes sure we are arriving safely. Thankfully, we will make it and we were here!

Speech punctuation 1

unit 6

 Key idea

When spoken words are written down, they are called **direct speech**. They need special marks to separate them from the rest of a sentence. They are called **speech marks**.

speech marks   speech marks

"I am far too busy," said Anton.

Speech marks are placed in front of the first word spoken, and after the last word spoken. Try to remember that:

• The first spoken word begins with a capital letter.
• A new paragraph is begun for each speaker.
• Spoken and non-spoken words are separated by a punctuation mark, for example, a comma, a question mark or an exclamation mark.

"Can I go out now?" asked Alysha.
"No, you can't!" said Mum.

Top Tip

Speech marks work in sets: once you have opened them, you must remember to close them.

Try it out!

Write out these sentences. Put in the missing speech marks. The first one has been done for you. *(2 marks for each correct sentence)*

1 This is your new sister, said Mum.
   "This is your new sister," said Mum.
2 Oh yes, said Anton, hardly bothering to look up from his computer game.
3 Have a good look at her, encouraged Dad.

12

Write out these sentences. Put in the missing speech marks and capital letters. *(2 marks for each correct sentence)*

4 a computer game can wait, moaned Dad.
5 Anton explained, but I'm nearly through level four.
6 is that good? asked Gran.

Keep practising! •

Use these non-spoken words in sentences containing direct speech. Include speech marks and capital letters. *(2 marks for each sentence)*

1 … shouted Anton crossly.

2 … Dad asked Mum.

3 … Mum answered.

4 … asked Gran.

5 Anton replied …

Take up the challenge! •

This writer has made mistakes with speech marks, capital letters and other punctuation marks. Find the twenty mistakes and write the story correctly. *(0.5 mark for each correct answer)*

What shall we do about Anton? asked Dad. "He could get worse. I think he is starting to look at her," said Mum. I saw him peeping over the screen of his computer.

Dad said, how can we get him really interested?

Got it shouted Mum. We'll take a digital photograph. I'll do that piped up Gran.

The next day Anton shouted, guess who is in my computer game? I've found my sister on Level Five!

Devices for presenting text

🔑 Key idea

Text can be organised and presented in different ways. This can make it easier for the reader to understand.

It is important that information text is easy to understand.

Different **devices** can be used to make the reader look at particular words.

new font

Some **materials** are **manufactured**.   bold

Some materials are <u>manufactured</u>.   underlined

- You can use a different font, underline words or make them bold and bigger.
- Headings and subheadings can be added to organise the text into different sections.
- Captions and speech bubbles attract the reader's attention.

Non-fiction books are most likely to use a range of these devices.

LATEST CLOTHES HIT SHOPS!

Shoppers flood into children's sports shops to buy **Beepa's** latest kit. WHY? Because their clothes are:

• Cheap! • Colourful! • Practical! • PLASTIC!

Beepa has produced the first *all-plastic* range of clothes.

Let **Beepa** answer your worries:

Q What happens when the clothes get dirty?

A Just hose your child down.

Q What happens when the clothes get too small?

A We can melt down and recycle them for you.

Remember the three **convincing** features:

1 factory-made 2 hard but soft 3 man-made

BUY NOW!

Try it out!

The notice on page 14 is in today's newspaper. Identify eight devices for presenting text. Say which two you think are the most effective and why they work well. *(10 marks)*

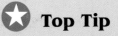
Keep practising!

This text could be improved with the use of some presentational devices. Write it out, adding ten presentational devices which the reader may find helpful. *(10 marks)*

When was plastic first used?

Plastic was first made in America early in the 20th century.

Why is plastic popular now?

There are many advantages to this material. It is very light, so items made from it are manageable for people with physical handicaps. It is easy to care for. No special cleaning preparations are needed: just soap and water are adequate.

What about the future?

The world will not run out of plastic. Plastic is a man-made material, so more can always be made in a factory.

Take up the challenge!

Make up your own piece of writing for the class newspaper. It can be about a sport or local activity. Use ten helpful presentational devices. Using a computer would be helpful. *(10 marks)*

Assessment 1

Sentences

The writer has forgotten the rules for the start and the end of a sentence. See if you can correct them. *(1 mark for each correct sentence)*

1 after the weekend, Mr Perkins went into the classroom
2 he had become a different person
3 of course, Class 3 did not know that
4 they just thought he was their same timid teacher
5 then strange things started to happen

Question marks and exclamation marks

Some of these sentences end in a ? and some in an ! You decide.

(1 mark for each correct answer)

1 Listen to that
2 What a shock it was
3 Who could believe it
4 When did Mr Perkins last raise his voice
5 What was happening to Wayne Beaker

Using commas in a list

Write sentences listing what you would find in the places shown below. Include at least three things in each list. Separate the last two items in each list with a word such as *and*. How will you separate the other items? *(1 mark for each sentence)*

1 your pencil case   2 your bag for a weekend trip
3 your bedroom   4 your school bag
5 your ideal Christmas stocking

Verbs in sentences

One of the boys was not listening when Mr Perkins taught verbs. He has forgotten how to use them! Can you make these into complete sentences for him? *(1 mark for each sentence)*

1 Something weird _____ in this class.
2 The children _____ strange things.
3 My best friend, Wayne, _____ on a chair.
4 My other friend, Lee, _____ all the answers to the test.
5 A stranger _____ into the classroom at 9 o'clock.

Verb tenses

Now the same boy is using the wrong tense. Correct the sentences for him using the tense shown in brackets. *(1 mark for each sentence)*

1 The stranger will arrive last Monday. *(past)*
2 He will be a school inspector from the government. *(past)*
3 Today was his last day in school. *(present)*
4 By tomorrow he has gone. *(future)*
5 Tomorrow the teacher breathed a sigh of relief. *(future)*

Speech punctuation 1

Rewrite these sentences using all the special punctuation rules for direct speech.*(1 mark for each sentence)*

1 Mr Perkins said I want everyone to be quiet.
2 One boy whispered not me.
3 Then Mr Perkins repeated everyone, please be quiet.
4 I'm not being quiet muttered Wayne Beaker.
5 Be quiet thundered Mr Perkins.

Presenting text in different ways

Choose a piece of your writing and think of ways to improve the presentation. Then write it out – you could use a computer.

unit 9

Adjectives 1

 Key idea

An adjective describes something or somebody within a sentence.

adjective   adjective

The young boy is exhausted.

- Adjectives describe nouns and pronouns.
- Adjectives may come before a noun or after a verb.
- Adjectives may be grouped according to their meaning, for example:
  number: five, seven, thousand
  size: big, little, long
  colour: red, grey, multicoloured
  mood: angry, sad, happy
  sense: smelly, pretty, loud.

 Top Tip

In order to check if a word is an adjective, ask yourself who or what it describes.

Try it out! •

Find, and write out, the adjective in each sentence.

(2 marks for each correct answer)

1 It was a long trip from home.
2 Melissa missed the noisy bustle of London.
3 A man in green uniform spoke to her.
4 "You'll love staying with kind
   Mrs Grimes," he said.
5 Mrs Grimes had a grim expression.

Work with a partner to find the adjectives and the nouns they are describing. The first one is done for you. *(1 mark for each correct answer)*

1. Mrs Grimes did not have **kind ways.**
   adjective = *kind*, noun = *ways*
2. She gave Melissa the worst room in the house.
3. It had a low ceiling.   5. It had horrible wallpaper.
4. It had cold floors.   6. At home, Melissa had a comfortable room.

Take up the challenge!

Many adjectives can be grouped together. For example, *miniscule* and *huge* could be grouped under "size".

Read this story and find twenty adjectives. Copy out the chart and add the adjectives under the right groupings. *(0.5 mark for each adjective)*

size	colour	mood	age
big	blue	angry	ancient

The old, faded wallpaper made sure that Melissa did not feel lonely; but it was upsetting company. It seemed friendly enough – dark trees and bushes with orange and green leaves. Berries were painted: tiny, red dots thrown haphazardly on the boring design. However, that was only the scene during the short period of light in the room; it was the night that seemed never-ending. In the evening, the leaves took on new, menacing forms, and Melissa reverted to being a little girl. She knew she was being silly, but the leaves became yellowing faces; the berries became the crimson spots of measles; and Melissa felt afraid of the long hours ahead of her.

Adjectives 2

 Key idea

Adjectives need to be chosen and used carefully to make them effective. Look at the sentence below.

adjective   adjective

The struggling teacher had an original idea to please the inspector.

Original tells the reader that the idea is new; **struggling** says that the teacher is having difficulty doing her job.

• Adjectives should add new information to the sentence.
• It is usually best not to repeat the same adjectives.
• Adjectives are most effective when used sparingly.

> ⭐ **Top Tip**
> When you use an adjective, check that the noun being described does not already contain that information.

Try it out! ·

In the sentence below there is at least one adjective that does not add new information. Find the adjective and write it down. *(2 marks for each correct answer)*

1 Mrs Grimes's cold house was full of strange, odd objects.
   Delete strange or odd – they both have the same meaning.

2 There were unattractive vases and old antiques everywhere.

3 They made Melissa anxious and worried.

4 Mrs Grimes did not want her own, personal belongings to be touched by a careless child.

5 Melissa was terrified that she would have an unintentional accident.

6 Melissa made up her mind not to touch one single thing.

The writer knows that this text is short of adjectives. He has left gaps for you to fill. *(1 mark for each correct answer)*

Every day, Melissa was in _____ danger of a hand, foot or arm knocking something. Mrs Grimes kept a _____ watch on her during the whole time she was in the house. The school day was a _____ relief to Melissa, but the long weekends were _____. The days seemed _____. The house was cold, and Melissa felt constantly _____. Really it was _____ that something would happen. It was almost as if Mrs Grimes was just waiting for this _____ event. One Tuesday morning, a _____ day, Melissa got up as usual at 7 o'clock. She hurried, as punctual meal times were _____ to Mrs Grimes, and breakfast was at 7.20 a.m. sharp.

The writer wrote this passage in a rush. In pairs, improve and rewrite this part of his story. Think about:
- **replacing some of the adjectives with better ones**
- **taking out some of the adjectives that are not needed**
- **replacing some of the nouns with better ones.** *(10 marks)*

Melissa hurried out of her small, tiny room at the highest top of the unpleasant, dislikeable house. She made her fast, hurried way down the first lot of stairs. Here there was not a big, roomy lot of space. Melissa was always good, sensible and well-behaved with the house things here. However, today was not the same as usual. She was worried and anxious about being late and unpunctual for breakfast. Then the bad thing happened! She gave an accidental hit against a big, large, vase with patterns on it. There was a nasty, horrible noise! The vase began to roll down the stairs.

unit 11

Plurals 1

🔑 Key idea

Nouns can be singular or plural. Most nouns add **s** or **es** to form the plural.

> singular noun   plural noun   plural noun

     The man owned two farms near churches.

There are also many irregular plural nouns.

> irregular plural noun

     The men owned two houses.

Some nouns exist in only the plural form, for example, **news** and **scissors**.

Try to remember that:
- Most nouns have different singular and plural forms.
- Most nouns add **s** or **es** to form the plural.
- There are many exceptions.

> ⭐ **Top Tip**
>
> Try saying the plural form. If you can hear an extra syllable, think about adding **es**.

Try it out! •

These are all singular nouns. Write their plural forms. Watch out – some of them are irregular! *(0.5 mark for each correct answer)*

school	lunch	box	goose
jelly	window	strawberry	sandwich
mouse	donkey	baby	sheep
shoe	antenna	deer	child
church	fox	scarf	rain

Copy out the chart for different types of plurals. Make a list of at least four plural nouns under each heading. You need a total of twenty plurals, and you are allowed to take only three words from **Try it out!** *(0.5 mark for each correct answer)*

regular plurals ending in s or es	irregular plurals	same in both singular and plural
hands	children	sheep

Amjit went on an outing to a farm. She had to write about it. She seems to have forgotten her plurals! Find her twenty mistakes and fix them. *(0.5 mark for each correct answer)*

What a fabulous day! We went on two busss to Wixden Farm. I have always lived in citys, so I am not used to being near lots of fieldes and animals. We saw so much: deers, chickens, sheeps, lambes, piges, goats and donkeys. We went into one of the paddockes, where we were allowed to stroke the horses and poneys. The only thing that I did not like was the flys!

Later we were allowed to explore the farm: I found four rabbites, three cockerel, and two dogs with their babeys. After that my friend and I climbed over two stile into a field where there were some cattles. Unfortunately, I forgot to put my wellies on, so my best trouser got covered in mud. After we had eaten our sandwichs in one of the fieldss, I sneaked back for one last look at the puppys. The farmer saw me looking at them, and he offered me one of them. It was not easy new to break to Mum!

Plurals 2

🔑 Key idea

When a singular noun is changed to the plural, other words in the sentence may change. For example, verbs are likely to change.

> singular noun   verb

The fire was lit in the field.
The fires were lit in the field.

> plural noun   verb

Pronouns that refer to the nouns may also change, for example:

> singular noun   pronoun

The fire was lit in the field; it burned brightly.
The fires were lit in the field; they burned brightly.

> plural noun   pronoun

Try it out! •

Choose the correct form of the verb. Write the complete sentence.

(2 marks for each correct answer)

1 The Class 3 children _____ the trip to Dorset. *enjoy/enjoys*
2 Two girls _____ the chance to go in a helicopter. *gets/get*
3 Four boys _____ a dingy with an instructor. *sail/sails*
4 The whole class _____ one special activity. *does/do*
5 The teacher now _____ one more night left on the trip. *have/has*

 Top Tip
Think about matching nouns and verbs. Are they both singular or plural?

These sentences are in the plural. Find and underline the two words in each sentence which show this. Remember to look at nouns, pronouns and verbs. There is one trick sentence which is not in the plural. Can you find it? *(0.5 mark for each correct answer and 1 mark for the trick sentence)*

1 Some dormitories are converted barns.
2 They have strange names.
3 Darren and Jason are in charge of the two barn dormitories.
4 They both hate being out of the main building.
5 The barn dormitories are draughty.
6 The barn doors rattle.
7 They swing open in windy weather.
8 The doors lock from the inside.
9 Six boys and Darren sleep in Cattleshed Barn.
10 Darren's door is locked from the inside.

Take up the challenge! ●

Make the nouns and pronouns underlined into plurals. You need to make sure the verbs match too. Be careful – you may not need to change everything! *(0.5 mark for each correct answer)*

The barn <u>door</u> opens from the inside only. For safety, the <u>boy</u> is not given any <u>key</u>. <u>He</u> is not trusted. Only the <u>teacher</u> knows how to be careful with the <u>lock</u>. The <u>dormitory</u> has <u>its</u> own fire <u>alarm</u>. <u>It</u> makes a noise like a siren. The fire <u>alarm</u> is very powerful and <u>it</u> goes off easily. Nobody ignores the sirens.

More uses of capital letters

🔑 Key idea

Capital letters are used for the start of a sentence and for other special words.

> It had been a long Friday at Longhaul Residential Centre, and Darren was very tired.

- Days and months begin with capital letters: Monday, May.
- All the words in the name of a place begin with a capital: Reed Primary School.
- I on its own is always a capital letter.
- Initials are usually in capitals: Mrs F H Brown.

Capital letters are also useful for headings and special emphasis.

Try it out! •

Two capital letters are missing from every sentence. Find the places and write the sentences correctly. *(0.5 mark for each correct answer)*

1 by 9.30 darrren was completely exhausted.
2 he was desperate to get to his room in cattleshed Barn.
3 On saturday he would be back in his flat in London road.
4 the thought of leaving longhaul was welcome.
5 After all, he had worked far harder than jason or miss Doyle.
6 Finally, once the boys were asleep, he locked cattleshed barn.
7 class 3's student teacher, darren, collapsed into bed.
8 it was too late to hang up the key as darren was too tired.
9 In a minute, he was sleeping the sleep of sleeping beauty.
10 all was silent at longhaul apart from the howl of the wind.

There are lots of signs at Longhaul Residential Centre. They include lots of capital letters. Add to these notices, using at least ten more capitals. *(1 mark for each correct answer)*

WET FLOOR!

What's happening
this week?
Monday – archery

Local Facilities
Post Office on Vicarage Rd

LONGHAUL RULES
Walk on the paths.
Do not ...

DUTY ROTA
Darren –

This sign is in the dormitory. Make it easier to understand by putting some of the sentences on new lines. You also need to add in some more capital letters. (You need to add at least twenty capitals.) *(0.5 mark for each correct answer)*

Be SaFe always hang the key up at night. Do noT leave the key in your pocket. do nOt lie with your head close to the alarm. Keep a copy of the booklet, cattleshed survival, close to you at all times. if you get trapped inside cattleshed, just shout through the door cracks. After that, think about waving a copy of longhaul times at the window. finally, jump up and down waving something red. kEep calM

unit 14

Words – do we need all of them?

Sentences include words that help them make sense. Without these words, the sentence won't make sense! Look at this sentence:

The exhausted teacher slept peacefully in the dormitory.

The important words in this sentence are the noun (**teacher**) and the verb (**slept**). The sentence will sound very strange without them!

However, you can take away the describing words (**exhausted, peacefully**). The sentence will still make sense.

The teacher slept in the dormitory.

The is called a determiner. Words like this do not really add to the meaning of the sentence. However, if you take these words away, the sound of the sentence changes.

Prepositions such as **in** and **on** need to stay, unless the phrase that goes with them is also taken away (**in** the dormitory).

Try it out! ·

 Top Tip

When taking words away, try reading out the new sentence. Have you kept the meaning?

Save words: pick one word you do not need in each sentence. The first one is done for you.

(1 mark for each correct answer)

1 Darren was <u>quite</u> exhausted.
2 The room was very hot.
3 Darren had closed every single window.
4 He lay absolutely still.
5 He fell into sweet dreams.

6 He pictured his peaceful flat.
7 He dreamed of chocolate cake.

Keep practising! •

Find and write the nouns and verbs which are essential to meaning. There are two in each sentence. *(1 mark for each correct answer)*

1 No sound came from the outdoor dormitory.
   noun = sound, verb = came
2 Suddenly, a change happened in Cattleshed Barn.
3 A loud, piercing noise burst from the fire alarm.
4 The children jumped in their beds.
5 Darren lay still in his deep sleep.
6 Boys leaped from every bunk in the children's section.
7 Slowly but surely, panic showed on the faces of the boys.

Take up the challenge! •

Make these shorter, but keep the same meaning. Leave out at least two or three words. The first one is done for you.
(2 marks for each sentence)

1 Harry, having the loudest voice, did the shouting.
   Harry did the shouting.
2 The careless, sleeping teacher didn't hear him.
3 Of course, the six trapped boys grew more and more frantic.
4 With eagle eyes, Jack saw the safety instructions on the wall!
5 Immediately, he rushed to read every single word
   of the important instructions.
6 The others listened carefully and attentively.
7 Then they started to take quick, immediate action.

unit 15

Using the first, second and third person

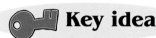
Key idea

A verb and pronoun need to match.

- Pronouns mark the person used.
- Persons can be singular or plural (**I** or **we**).
- Different types of texts are written in different persons.

The second person is used in commands. Command verbs do not need their pronoun (**you**), for example:

Give it here! Go outside. Take your coat with you.

Try it out! ●

All these sentences are in the third person except for one which is in the second person. Find the pronouns and the verbs that go with them. Say which person is being used. *(1 mark for each correct sentence)*

1 She stares in horror at the pieces of broken vase.
   pronoun = she, third person, verb = stares

2 She watches Mrs Grimes.

3 She too is staring at her favourite vase.

4 They seem too shocked to speak.

5 They are silent.

6 Then she hears the sharp words.

7 "You come here! Now!"

8 She stumbles her way downstairs.

9 She starts to help Mrs Grimes gather the pieces of broken china.

10 They pick up the pieces together.

11 It is a long job.

 Top Tip

Speaking is as important as writing. Read your writing aloud to a partner. You will be able to hear if it doesn't sound right.

Keep practising!

Look again at the sentences in Try it out! Then rewrite them in the first person (I or we). You can leave out sentences 7 and 11. Be careful with pronouns and verb forms, but watch out for other necessary changes. The first one is done for you. *(1 mark for each correct sentence and 2 extra marks if you get them all right!)*

1 She stares in horror at the pieces of broken vase.
   I stare in horror at the pieces of broken vase.

Take up the challenge!

My story is a mess! I want it to be in the third person, using *she* or *they*, but I have made lots of mistakes. Find and fix my twenty wrong words. *(0.5 mark for each correct answer)*

Melissa keeps quiet. I am afraid to speak. I say nothing. I dare not say the wrong thing. They continues to gather up every piece. We searches the carpet for tiny fragments. We goes to the floor edges with our fingertips. We both knows that every fragment is needed. It are the only way that the vase can be made whole again. Melissa watch as Mrs Grimes carry the pieces of vase into the kitchen.
They is placed on the table. Then I fetch the glue.

Assessment 2

Adjectives

Choose the best adjective from the box to complete the sentence. Try to use a different adjective each time. *(0.5 mark for each correct answer)*

strange	interesting	croaky	new	peculiar	red	tiny
white	similar	special	grey	crooked	different	
mysterious	quiet	short	enormous	loud	long	hoarse

1 _____ things were happening in Class 3.
2 The children were definitely _____.
3 One boy spoke in a _____ whisper.
4 He used to have a _____ voice.
5 James Kindle used to have _____ legs.
6 However, by Wednesday he took very _____ steps.
7 Wayne Beaker's hair turned _____.
8 Poor Lee had become too _____ for his chair.
9 He had to have _____ furniture from a different class.
10 What _____ power did Mr Perkins have?

Plurals

Make the nouns underlined plural. Watch out for other changes you might need to make. *(0.5 mark for each correct answer)*

The <u>child</u> in Class 3 keeps disappearing! Their <u>parent</u> is distraught. The <u>teacher</u> of all the other <u>class</u> is baffled. The other <u>pupil</u> wants to stay at home.
<u>Size</u> is becoming a real problem. Some <u>boy</u> keeps falling off the <u>chair</u>: even the nursery <u>chair</u> is too big. The school <u>uniform</u> looks silly: the <u>jumper</u> is trailing on the floor, and the <u>shoe</u> flop around like a <u>boat</u>. The <u>problem</u> just grows worse.

Other uses of capital letters

You are a Class 3 pupil whose dog has gone missing. Write a notice, appealing for information. Remember to use capital letters for:
- the first letter of a sentence
- headings
- names of people, places, days and months
- emphasis. *(5 marks)*

Words – do we need all of them?

A journalist has written this article but the Editor says it is too long. Take out some words to make the article shorter. Try to find eight words or phrases that you can cut. *(1 mark for each correct answer)*

Shrinkage!

Local, nearby schoolchildren are shrinking! Parents are struggling to keep their children dressed in clothes which fit and are the right size. Many of the parents are not wealthy or rich. Having to buy more and more clothes is expensive and costly.

Some of the local doctors wonder if a bad, unhealthy diet is to blame. Others say that the water supply could be doing it and could be to blame. Together, everyone in the area is extremely worried and bothered. Some children are already getting very near to tiny toddler sizes. Something must be done at once.

Using the first, second and third person

In the sentences below, the pronouns and verbs don't match. Find the verbs and change them. Which pronoun does each one match?
(1 mark for each correct answer)

1 She are not pleased with the article.
2 I writes far too many words.
3 We works together to change it.
4 "You has to make it better," they say.
5 At last he says that he are happy.

unit 17

Pronouns 1

🔑 Key idea

Pronouns stand in place of common and proper nouns.

> noun Jaye really liked football. noun
>
> pronoun She really liked it. pronoun

Pronouns often refer to people, for example:

> Jamil = **he** Mrs Agathou = **she**

Using a pronoun means you don't have to keep repeating the same name, for example:

> noun Jamil had homework. noun
>
> pronoun He wanted to do it quickly. pronoun

⭐ Top Tip

Use a pronoun that saves words but keeps the meaning clear.

Try it out! • • • • • • • • • • • • • • • • • • •

Find the pronouns in these sentences. Say which nouns they are replacing. The first one has been done for you.

(1 mark for each correct answer)

1 Jamil had piano lessons which he hated.
   Jamil = noun, he = pronoun

2 Mrs Patel gave the lessons and she was strict.

3 The lessons started at 2 o'clock and they lasted two hours.

4 The lesson was on Saturday, and it really spoilt the day.

5 Football was more fun, and Jamil was good at it.

6 Jamil had to play the same tune and he did not enjoy the music.

7 When Jamil and his friend were talking, they had an idea.

1 Match up the nouns with the correct pronouns. (More than one pronoun might match each noun.) *(1 mark for each correct answer)*

nouns		pronouns	
furniture	girl	they	it
father	parents	them	her
brother	grandparents	them	it
belongings	accident	he	she
mother	London	it	him

2 Test your answers on a partner. Make up two sentences using the noun and the pronoun you have chosen to match it. For example:

The furniture is too big. **It** is going back to the shop.
Does your partner understand who or what the pronoun refers to?

Save words, but still keep the meaning clear. Find ten places where you can change nouns for pronouns. *(1 mark for each correct answer)*

1 When Jamil and Jaz talked, Jamil and Jaz planned what to do.
2 Mrs Patel and Jamil were alone when Mrs Patel and Jamil worked.
3 Mrs Patel looked at the piano, keeping her eyes on the piano.
4 Mrs Patel listened to the music to hear mistakes in the music.
5 The teacher did not see a machine, as the machine was hidden.
6 When Jamil moved his fingers, Jamil pressed the machine with his foot.
7 Music played and the music sounded wonderful.
8 Jamil's fingers moved, so the teacher thought Jamil's fingers were making the music.

unit 18

Pronouns 2

Key idea

Possessive pronouns are linked to personal pronouns. They both replace nouns. However, they each do a different job in a sentence.

personal pronoun

He liked the new toy.
He argued that the toy was his.

personal pronoun   possessive pronoun

- Possessive pronouns show ownership.
- Pronouns and verbs must match.

> ## ⭐ Top Tip
> When you use a pronoun, make sure it matches the noun.

Try it out! •

Choose the correct possessive pronouns to fill these gaps. *(2 marks for each correct answer)*

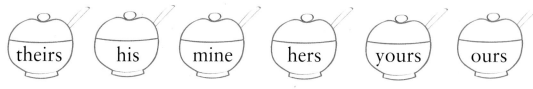

theirs   his   mine   hers   yours   ours

1 Craig bought the cake, so he decided it was _____.
2 His sister argued that it was _____.
3 In fact, the money was for both of them, so the cake was really _____ to share.
4 Still Craig carried on shouting, "It's _____!"
5 "How can it be _____ if the money was between us?" said his sister.
6 "Really, the cake is _____, " she said.

Replace the underlined words below with pronouns. Use the chart
to help you choose the best pronoun. *(2 marks for each correct answer)*

personal pronouns		possessive pronouns	
singular	plural	singular	plural
I	we	mine	ours
you	you	yours	yours
he	they	his	theirs
she		hers	
it		its	

Craig just would not give in about the cake, and <u>Craig</u> kept
shouting, "The cake is <u>my cake</u>!"

"It's <u>owned by us</u>," said Sharon, very fairly.

"It's <u>owned by me</u>," insisted Craig, unfairly.

"Who gave you the money, Craig?" Mum asked.

"Dad," <u>Craig</u> replied.

"Then the cake is <u>Dad's property</u>!" said Mum.

**There are eight verbs here that do not agree with their pronouns.
You need to find them and change them.** *(1 mark for each correct answer)*

Craig are hungrier than ever now. However, he soon get an idea:
Sharon will "give" him some of her chocolate! After all, with a bar
of chocolate that size, it am definitely big enough for two.

Sharon is reading a book, so she do not hear Craig's footsteps.

"Boo!" he shout as he claps his hands.

The chocolate flies out of her hands, it land on the floor, and two
pieces snap off. In a second, they is in Craig's mouth. He race off
leaving Sharon wailing.

Speech punctuation 2

 Key idea

In writing, speech marks are placed around the words that are spoken. There are special punctuation rules to follow too.

> "Will anyone hear us?" asked Liam.
> "I hope so," said Jack.
> Harry shouted, "Don't waste time!"

- The first spoken word begins with a capital letter.
- A comma, question mark, or exclamation mark separates the spoken words (direct speech) from the rest of the sentence.
- You need to start a new line when someone else starts to speak.

Try it out! •

Rewrite these sentences and put in the missing speech marks. *(1 mark for each correct sentence)*

1 I'll wave the newspaper, said Josh.
2 Help is needed in Cattleshed Barn, shouted Harry.
3 Josh, can't you jump higher? demanded Jack.
4 I can't carry on, wheezed Josh.
5 Who else wants to try? Jack shouted.
6 George, the tallest, announced, It had better be me.
7 Just get on with it! yelled Harry.
8 I wish I'd brought my United football top, muttered Liam.
9 Rupal said, My red handkerchief is the best thing we've got.
10 Harry went on screaming, Come and get us!

 Top Tip
Read the sentence aloud and use a different voice for the spoken words. Then put speech marks around those words.

Make up a sentence for each boy. Use the phrase in the speech bubble. Remember, you need to separate the "speech" (spoken words) from the rest of the sentence. Use speech marks and punctuation to help you do this. *(2 marks for each sentence)*

Ten punctuation marks are missing in the sentences. Identify the places and copy out the text correctly. *(1 mark for each correct answer)*

1 "We need to make more noise, said Jack.
2 I think I'm losing my voice," said Harry. "Can anyone else take over?
3 Liam muttered, I'll have a go."
4 "How could your voice be heard sneered Rupal.
5 Stop arguing screamed Josh. "I'll take over.

Conjunctions

🔑 Key idea

A conjunction is a word that joins two
short sentences together to make a longer one.

conjunction

The boys were doing their best and they were working hard.

Conjunctions that are used a lot include:
and, but, because, or, so, if, while, then, so that, when, though

Try it out! ● ● ● ● ● ● ● ● ● ● ● ● ● ● ● ● ● ●

⭐ Top Tip

Try not to use **and** too
much. Other conjunctions
may be better.

Find the conjunction in each sentence.

(1 mark for each correct answer)

1   The boys kept up their efforts, though they were feeling weary.
2   George leaped high into the air while he waved the handkerchief.
3   Liam kept thinking about his United football top, and he wished
    he had brought the red jersey.
4   Joe's arm ached but he waved a copy of *Longhaul Times*.
5   Jack kept up a stream of praise because it was all he could do.
6   He was calling out cheerful words, while he was beginning to
    feel despair.
7   He did not think he could keep the boys going if help did not
    come soon.
8   He kept a smile on his face so that the others would not give up.
9   When they had tried everything, there was nothing else to do.
10 Was he right or was he wrong?

conjunctions

because   so that
while   though   and

Choose a sentence from B to match up with a sentence from A.
Join them together with one of the conjunctions from the box.
When you have finished you should have five longer sentences.
(2 marks for each sentence)

A
Darren, the student teacher,
  began to stir
Rupal noticed this
Everyone stopped
Jack was relieved
He had been in charge

B
they could look at Darren
the boys were so noisy
he also felt angry
Darren was asleep
he told everyone to be quiet

Take up the challenge! •

Ten conjunctions have been underlined. Choose a new conjunction
from the box to replace each one. *(1 mark for each correct answer)*

and	but	yet	so	when	then	and	while	or	because

Darren stirred again <u>because</u> only his head moved. The boys
gasped <u>so that</u> the student teacher yawned. He opened one eye,
<u>when</u> he opened his other eye two seconds later. He sat up
carefully <u>but</u> he held on to edge of the bed. He rubbed his side <u>or</u> it
was aching. Was he dreaming <u>though</u> were all the boys staring at
him? His side really hurt <u>then</u> the bed felt comfortable. He saw a
small hole in the mattress <u>if</u> he could see something shining in it.
He pulled out a piece of metal <u>yet</u> the boys gasped. It was the
missing key <u>because</u> they were safe!

unit 21

Time words and phrases

 **Key idea**

Time words or groups of time words (**phrases**) tell you when something is happening. They can be used at the start of the sentence:

At first it was impossible to wake Paul. **Later** he began to stir.

- Time words can make a **connection** between sentences, for example, She was tired but **earlier** she had been very lively.
- Time words can help you to understand the order in which things happen.
- Time words are a quick way to give you more information.

Try it out! . . . .

Underline the time words and phrases in these sentences. *(1 mark for each correct answer)*

1 First, the alarm clock went off.
2 At this point I thought I was dreaming of an explosion.
3 Once I realised what was happening, I opened just one eye.
4 Next, I opened the other eye.
5 After a while, I sat up.
6 Only then did I realise how late I was.
7 Immediately, I jumped out of bed.
8 Meanwhile, my mum was shouting at me to come down for breakfast.
9 Eventually, I made it downstairs.
10 Next time, I will get up as soon as the clock rings!

 Top Tip

If you keep writing "and then", it can sound boring. Look for more interesting connections.

Fill the gaps in the sentences. Choose the time words (or phrases) from the clock. *(2 marks for each correct answer)*

Finally
Next   Immediately
First   Meanwhile

1 _____, Paul thought he was dreaming.
2 _____, he realised that it was morning.
3 _____, he hopped out of bed.
4 _____, the smell of breakfast wafted up the stairs.
5 _____, he tucked into his breakfast.

Write a set of five rules to ensure that you get up on time and are not late for school. Choose a different time word or phrase from the backpack to start each sentence. *(2 marks for each rule)*

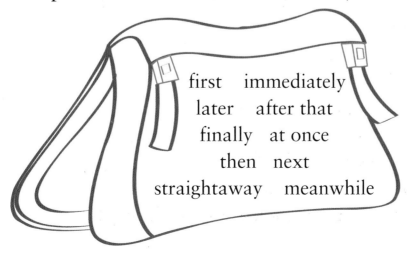

first   immediately
later   after that
finally   at once
then   next
straightaway   meanwhile

More commas

 **Key idea**

Commas are used to break up sentences. They help us to understand what the sentence means.

> comma   comma   comma
>
> Frank, at last, was going to get a dog. However, he still had to choose it.

Adverbs like **meanwhile**, **suddenly**, **however** and **therefore** often need a comma after them too.

> adverb and comma
>
> Meanwhile, Mum was deciding which dog rescue home to visit.
> Frank, however, already knew which one.
>
> adverb and comma

> ⭐ **Top Tip**
> Commas may be used in pairs.

> ⭐ **Top Tip**
> Read your writing aloud. Now try to match your punctuation to the way you said it.

Try it out! • • • • • • • • • • • • • • • • • • •

Put the two missing commas in each of these sentences. (*2 marks for each correct answer*)

1　Frank thanks to Mum was going to get a puppy.
2　His two friends Sam and Ravi said they would help him choose.
3　Frank still amazed by his luck was very excited.
4　His Dad as Frank knew wasn't too sure about the puppy.
5　His Mum who loved dogs was even more excited than Frank!

Each of these sentences contains an adverb that needs a comma (or commas) to separate it from the rest of the sentence. Find the adverbs, and add the commas. There are ten commas to add.
(1 mark for each correct answer)

1 Luckily Dad didn't try to spoil Frank's plans.
2 However he gave Frank lots of advice about choosing the right puppy.
3 Frank decided therefore that he had better listen.
4 Eventually the day came when Frank could choose his dog.
5 He was therefore very excited!
6 Meantime he piled into the car with Sam and Ravi.
7 Eventually they arrived at the dogs' home.
8 Finally he could choose his puppy!

Ten commas have been missed out below. Find the places they should go. *(1 mark for each correct answer)*

A lady who seemed very kind took them to see the dogs. Lots of dogs most of them barking ran to meet them. Meanwhile Sam was stroking a friendly poodle. Ravi with a big grin was patting a little terrier. Suddenly Frank spotted a black labrador puppy. Immediately he knew that this was the dog for him. However Dad wasn't so sure about his choice when they got home!

Assessment 3

Pronouns 1

Match each noun to the pronoun which could replace it. *(1mark for each correct answer)*

nouns: children   mother   clothes   father   dinner
pronouns: her   they   it   them   he

Pronouns 2

Choose a possessive pronoun to fill each gap or to replace the words that have been underlined. The first one has been done for you.

(1 mark for each correct answer)

| mine | yours | his | hers | ours | theirs |

1 The book had Miss Crumble's name on it, so it was _____. *(hers)*
2 The jumper had Wayne Beaker's name on, so that must be _____.
3 The box of pens just said "BOYS", so the pens must be _____.
4 "It can belong to all of us, so it's _____."
5 "As you found it, it's _____!" said Wayne.
6 "And the last laugh will be <u>the one belonging to me</u>," muttered Mr Perkins under his breath.

Speech punctuation 2

Add the missing speech marks and punctuation marks to the sentences. *(1 mark for each correct sentence)*

1 "I'd like a word, Mr Perkins said Mr Davies after school.
2 Is there a problem" asked Mr. Perkins.
3 "Problem! Of course there is exploded the head teacher.
4 You're losing pupils. Where are they? the head teacher shouted.
5 I can't say for sure, stuttered Mr Perkins.

Conjunctions

Choose a conjunction from the box to join together each pair of sentences. *(1 mark for each correct answer)*

since	when	if	yet	or

1 Class 3 was getting smaller. There were fewer pupils daily.
2 Mr Perkins was a trained teacher. He still managed to lose pupils.
3 Parents started to panic. Their children shrank.
4 The mystery needed to be solved. Parents would move their children to another school.
5 The problem got worse. Mr Perkins would have to be sacked.

Time words and phrases

Here is a list of instructions. Put them in the right order. Underline the time word or phrase which is used in each sentence. *(1 mark for each correct answer)*

After that, keep measuring them each week.
First, measure your child and record their height.
Next, buy them a smaller school uniform.
Finally, keep them at home if they are less than 20 centimetres tall.
Then, measure them again a week later to see if they have shrunk.

More commas

These sentences are hard to understand. Add ten commas to help break them up. *(0.5 mark for each correct comma)*

1 The situation already terrible was getting worse.
2 Wayne Beaker now extremely tiny began to squeak.
3 Children laughed shouted and whistled all the time.
4 Consequently Mr Perkins became flustered.
5 The head teacher his head in his hands wept.
6 Nothing it seemed could be done.

Glossary

1st, 2nd, 3rd person
Different types of texts are written in different persons.
1st – *I skipped*   2nd – *you climb*   3rd – *she laughed*

adjective
A word or phrase that describes a noun – *The **young** girl is **exhausted**.*

comma
A punctuation mark that shows a pause in a sentence or separates items in a list.

conjunction
A linking word– *They ate their dinner **and** they went to bed.*

noun
A word that names a person, thing or feeling. Nouns can be **singular** (one – cat) or **plural** (more than one – cats).
- **proper nouns** name a specific person or thing – *Naomi, Manchester*
- **common nouns** name unspecific things – *child, apples*
- **collective nouns** name a group of people or things – *flock, audience*

pronoun
A word used in place of a noun – *Sam likes fruit. **He** likes apples best.*
- **personal pronouns** – *I, you, he, she, it, they, we, us, them*
- **possessive pronouns** – *my, mine, its, his, her, hers, our, ours, their, theirs*

speech marks ("...")
Punctuation marks used to show the actual words spoken when we write down speech – *Jack said, "I will climb the beanstalk."*

tense
The tense of a verb tells *when* the action is taking place.
- **past** tense (already happened) – *St George **fought** the dragon.*
- **present** tense (is happening now) – *St George **is fighting** the dragon.*
- **future** tense (will happen later) – *St George **will fight** the dragon.*

verb
A word (or words) that tells what is happening (the action) in a sentence – *The man **slurped** his soup. The man **was** noisy.*